Thank you to the generous team who gave their time and talents to make this book possible:

Authors
Ellenore Angelidis, Leyla Angelidis and Eyayu Genet

Illustrator
Eyayu Genet

Creative Directors
Caroline Kurtz, Jane Kurtz,
and Kenny Rasmussen

Translators
Yoseph Ayalew, Mastewal Abera,
Woubeshet Ayenew

Designer
Beth Crow

Ready Set Go Books, an Open Hearts Big Dreams Project

Special thanks to Ethiopia Reads donors and staff for believing in this project and helping get it started-- and for arranging printing, distribution, and training in Ethiopia.

ISBN: 979-8787005363
Library of Congress Control Number: 2021925382

Published: 12/20/21

Our Life is On the Lake

ሐይቁና ኑሯችን

English and Amharic

Lake Tana is a
huge and amazing
lake in Ethiopia.

የጣና ሐይቅ በኢትዮጵያ
የሚገኝ ትልቅና አስገራሚ
ሐይቅ ነው፡፡

The water from the lake
feeds big and small trees
that grow along its banks.

የሐይቁ ውኃ በዳርቻው የበቀሉ
ትላልቅና ትናንሽ ዛፎችን
ይመግባል፡፡

Hundreds of different
kinds of birds make their
homes on its shores.

በመቶዎች የሚቆጠሩ የተለያዩ
ዓይነት የአእዋፍ ዝርያዎች
መኖሪያቸውን በዳርቻው ላይ
ይሰራሉ።

Fish fill its waters
and feed those who
live nearby.

ውሃው በአሳዎች የተሞለ ነው
፤ አቅራቢያው የሚኖሩትንም
ይመግባል፨

Long ago, people learned
how to make boats.

በድሮ ግዜ ሰዎች ጀልባዎችን
እንዴት መስራት እንደሚችሉ
ተምረዋል፡፡

In those days, the castles
of Gondar rang with
songs and stories about
the amazing lake.

በእነዚያ ጊዜያት የጎንደር ቤተ
መንግስት ስለአስደናቂው ሐይቅ
በሚዜሙ ዜማዎች በሚነገሩ
ታሪኮች የተሞላ ነበር።

Over the centuries, the boats carried kings and queens, priests and ordinary people on the waters of Lake Tana.

ባለፉት ዘመናት ጀልባዎቹ በጣና ሐይቅ ውኃ ላይ ንጉሦችና፣ ንግሥቶችን፣ ካህናትን እና ሌሎችን ሰዎች ሲያመላልሱ ኖረዋል።

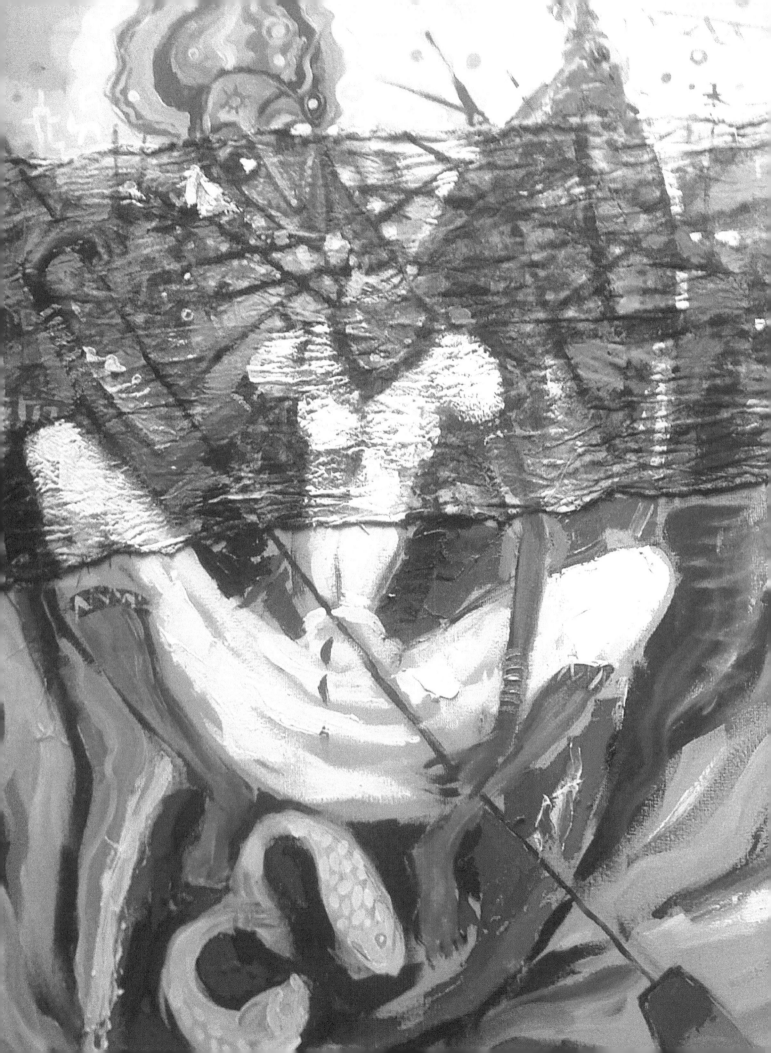

Church treasures were
stored on islands in
Lake Tana.

በጣና በሐይቅ ላይ ባሉ ደሴቶች
የቤተክርስቲያን ውድ ሃብቶች
ተከማችተዋል።

Today, people who come from many countries to visit the ancient cities of Ethiopia often start at Lake Tana.

ዛሬ ከብዙ ሀገራት የኢትዮጵያን ጥንታዊ ከተሞች ለመጎብኘት የሚመጡ ሰዎች ብዙን ግዜ ጉብኝታቸውን የሚጀምሩት ከጣና ሐይቅ ነው።

Parents teach the ways
of the lake, showing
their young ones how to
respect its traditions and
animal life.

ወላጆች ለልጆቻቸው የሐይቁን
ልማድና በውስጡ ያሉትን
እንስሳቶች አኗኗር እንዴት
ማክበር እንዳለባቸው በማሳየት
ሰለሐይቁ ያስተምሯቸዋል፡፡

People happily celebrate
the gifts they receive
from the lake.

ሰዎች ከሐይቁ በሚያገኙትን
ገጸበረከት ይደሰታሉ።

The sun's bright
reflection starts each
day with joy.

እያንዳንዱ ቀን በፀሐይዋ ብሩህ
ነጸብራቅ በደስታ ይጀመራል።

Our life is on the lake.

ኑሮዬችን ከሐይቁ ጋር
የተሳሰረ ነው፡፡

About the Story

This story was inspired when artist and co-author Eyayu posted all of his amazing paintings that feature Lake Tana and the life on and around it. Lake Tana is the largest lake in Ethiopia, fed by the Gilgel Abay, Reb and Gumara rivers. The river that people often call the Blue Nile flows out of Lake Tana to begin its long journey toward Egypt.

In 2015, the Lake Tana region was recognized by UNESCO for its national and international natural and cultural importance. In the many wetlands around Lake Tana, ancient plants like papyrus grow and birds can find food and build their nests. More than 217 different bird species have been recorded in the area. Each year, some birds leave their homes in Europe and Asia when the weather turns cold and spend part of the year on Lake Tana.

The lake is full of fish--67 different species—many of which live only in Ethiopia. It is also home to hippos. You can read about a real-life adventure with hippos on Lake Tana in another book by the same authors and illustrator, Surprise on Lake Tana. Both books show how important the area was in Ethiopia's history and how visitors can still see monasteries and churches dating back to the 13th century. In addition, many tourists who want to see ancient wonders in Axum and Gondar and Lalibela begin or end their trips in Bahir Dar on the shores of Lake Tana.

About the Author/Illustrator

Eyayu Genet is a visual artist and lecturer at Bahir Dar University. This book was inspired by his amazing paintings that depict life along Lake Tana and his inspiring words that are the title. He completed an MFA at Addis Ababa University and has exhibited his work in Ethiopia and various other places including Qatar, the United States, Sweden, Ecuador, and Uganda. He has been awarded  the Tana media award for his contributions to promote love and peace. He's engaged with many humanitarian and social programs and working to make Bahir Dar a showcase for art in Ethiopia.

About the Authors

Ellenore Angelidis is a public speaker, consultant, volunteer, lawyer, and aspiring writer. She stays busy with husband Michael and their three kids: two sons, Dimitri, Damian (who is an Open Hearts Big Dreams Junior Board member), and daughter, Leyla. Equalizing educational opportunities for children in Ethiopia is a passion that comes in part from being raised by two teacher parents and in part from raising an Ethiopian daughter. She founded and runs both OHBD and a new company L.E.A.D. (Lead Empower Activate Dream) LLC. Visiting Lake Tana and Bahir Dar has been a special highlight. Meeting and becoming friends with Eyayu Genet has led to amazing collaborations including three books. This is the first book where Eyayu Genet is also a co-author.

Leyla Marie Fasika Angelidis was born in Bahir Dar, Ethiopia and joined the Angelidis family in Seattle as an infant. She is currently in middle school and finds it unimaginable that some kids in her birth country don't get the chance to learn to read or go to school.

She has collaborated with her family to build a library in her birth town of Bahir Dar and to support other literacy projects through Open Hearts Big Dreams. She is an avid reader and aspiring writer. She has co-authored a number of OHBD Ready Set Go early reader books based on family experiences and personal interests. More recently, she is a featured spokesperson as well as helps with events and awareness building for OHBD literacy projects. Through these efforts she has learned more about her first country, language, and culture as well as positively contributed to her community in Ethiopia and in the US.

She has BIG DREAMS for herself and for kids living in Ethiopia (and around the world).

About Open Hearts Big Dreams

Open Hearts Big Dreams began as a volunteer organization, led by Ellenore Angelidis in Seattle, Washington, to provide sustainable funding and strategic support to Ethiopia Reads, collaborating with Jane Kurtz. OHBD has now grown to be its own nonprofit organization supporting literacy, innovation, and leadership for young people in Ethiopia.

Ellenore Angelidis comes from a family of teachers who believe education is a human right, and opportunity should not depend on your birthplace. And as the adoptive mother of a little girl who was born in Ethiopia and learned to read in the U.S., as well as an aspiring author, she finds the chance to positively impact literacy hugely compelling!

About Ready Set Go Books

Reading has the power to change lives, but many children and adults in Ethiopia cannot read. One reason is that Ethiopia doesn't have enough books in local languages to give people a chance to practice reading. Ready Set Go books wants to close that gap and open a world of ideas and possibilities for kids and their communities.

When you buy a Ready Set Go book, you provide critical funding to create and distribute more books.

Learn more at:
http://openheartsbigdreams.org/book-project/

About Ready Set Go Fine Art Series

We rely on volunteer artists and illustrators, including amateurs and some professionals. The French painter Henri Matisse said, "Creativity takes courage." We believe art has the power to help readers tap into their imagination and creativity at the same time as it helps reading comprehension.

Some of our professional artists have generously allowed us to use their paintings to act as illustrations in our books. We are launching this new series to show kids and adults the amazing work of some very talented, generous and creative people.

The series will feature artists from Ethiopia and around the globe.

About the Language

Amharic is a Semetic language -- in fact, the world's second-most widely spoken Semetic language, after Arabic. Starting in the 12th century, it became the Ethiopian language that was used in official transactions and schools and became widely spoken all over Ethiopia.

It's written with its own characters, over 260 of them. Eritrea and Ethiopia share this alphabet, and they are the only countries in Africa to develop a writing system centuries ago that is still in use today!

About the Translation

Yoseph Ayalew is a primary school teacher by training with a special interest in supporting the development of orphans and vulnerable children (OVC). In 2000 he founded a private school (MYFV Academy) offering kindergarten to grade 8 classes. MYFV provided a total of 54 FREE learning opportunities for orphans and vulnerable children; 15 of them funded by MYFV and 39 funded by an American NGO. In 2006, in collaboration with Volunteer Services Overseas (VSO), a UK NGO, Yoseph published his first children's book on HIV/AIDS. All books were distributed FREE to schools in Addis Ababa and throughout Ethiopia. In 2012, he published 2 books: "50 Answers to Children's Questions About HIV/AIDS" in collaboration with Ethiopia Reads, USA; and "The Loss of Innocence" in collaboration with People to People (P2P) Canada. Since 2011, Yoseph has been organizing a children's festival at the Addis Ababa Exhibition Center to celebrate the International Day of African Child.

Dr. Woubeshet Ayenew's role at Ready Set Go Books combines his passions for parenting and language. He is a cardiologist by training but parenting is his most demanding and wonderfully rewarding job. Once his children started to read and write in Amharic, he went out searching for child-friendly bilingual books. He eventually linked up with the creative team from Ready Set Go Books.

Though a resident of the US for over 30 years, he maintains a healthy grasp of his native language and culture; his shelves are filled with Amharic novels and other writings that he picks up during his regular medical mission trips to Ethiopia, and he assumes many roles in his Ethiopian community in Minnesota. He views every story in the Ready Set Go Books collection from the side of his Ethiopian-American children as well as from the perspective of the young readers of his native land. He knows the job is done when there is something wondrous for everyone in every story.

Over 100 unique Ready Set Go books available!

To view all available titles, search "Ready Set Go Ethiopia" or scan QR code

 Chaos

 Talk Talk Turtle

 We Can Stop the Lion

 Not Ready!

 Count For Me

 Too Brave

 Fifty Lemons

 The Glory of Gondar

Open Heart Big Dreams is pleased to offer discounts for bulk orders, educators and organizations.

Contact ellenore@openheartsbigdreams.org for more information.

CPSIA information can be obtained
at www.ICGtesting.com
Printed in the USA
LVHW070008040622
720468LV00002B/13